To Hell and Back

in a

Bottle

By: Buddy McNabb

Table of Contents

Chapter One - The Run That Would Change the Course of   3
My Life

Chapter Two – Family History   9

Chapter Three Reform School and Penitentiary   16

Chapter Four – Marriage and Divorce and Drinking   21

Chapter Five – The Army   31

Chapter Six – Flying Career   34

Chapter Seven – It's A Matter of Faith   37

Chapter Eight – The Musician   41

Chapter Nine – My Second Wife   43

Chapter Ten – Times When God Was With Me   50

Chapter Eleven – I Should Have Died…   55

Buddy McNabb Photo   61

Chapter One

The run that would change the course of my life.

In 1943, times were exciting. It was World War II. Everywhere you turned, there were signs of the war progressing. I thought I was grown at 13. I could have stayed but I chose to run away when I was in the sixth grade.

The choice I made that day changed the course of my life.

My brother and one of our friends made a pack that we would all run away together. However, when the time came as planned, we had a split second to decide if we would run or stay. Every day we would have the same routine. We always walked to school; but on this day, the principal just happened to be standing on the steps at the front door of the school. As we approached the school, my brother and his friend chickened out. But instead of focusing on the principal, I looked the other way and kept on walking.

I walked down West Main Street to a place called King's Night Club. I laid my books down in front of the Club and walked to the highway. I held my thumb up to hitchhike a ride; and to my surprise, a Lieutenant in the military stopped and picked me up. He was being stationed in Kentucky to 4th Ferring in Command. I said, "Hello, my name is Buddy McNabb. Where are you going?" He said, "I'm going to Memphis." I said, "I'm going where you are going."

Men were all in the military. Everyone was busy. Crime did not exist, except in organized crime. Machine Gun Kelly, notorious gangster, was captured in Memphis.

4

The Lieutenant took me to downtown Memphis. I got out of the car and stood in front of the Sterick Building in awe. On Madison and Third Avenue, I rode the elevator. I walked over to Front Street and looked over to the river. When I saw the Mississippi River, I thought it was the biggest thing I had ever seen. It makes the Tennessee River look like a creek.

I had three dollars and some change, and it was enough to buy me a burger. Then I walked to Confederate Park and laid down on a bench and went to sleep. It was in the springtime. When I got sleepy, I would just roll up my jacket and make me a pillow and go fast asleep.

The Park Bench in Memphis, TN

In those days there were police officers who walked a beat (a route). The cop on the beat tapped the bench with his baton, woke me up, and began asking me questions. He asked me if I had run away from home. I said, "Yes sir, I have." He told me, "If I take you to headquarters, they will send you back home. You know that, right?" He then asked if I would run away again. I said, "Yes sir, I will."

The police officer then took me to a parking garage at the corner of Court and Front Street which was open 24 hours per day. He knew the clerk, and he arranged a place for me to sleep on a couch. At 7 a.m. each morning when the police officer went off duty, he would come back and pick me up.

Before dark that first day, I had a job and a room in a boarding house at 1026 Poplar Street. It was a high dollar place to live – the cost was $6.00 per week. He took me to an employment office, and on their records, I was listed as age 18, but actually I was age 13. No documentation was required. I forged my guardian's name and my birthday.

During this time, there was such a great shortage of men working because most men were in the military. My first job was working as a mail clerk sorting mail. The kind police officer watched over me for about three months to make sure I was okay. Later, he then began checking on me periodically. He was a fine Christian man named Lewis.

In those days, people really did not focus on anyone's age. If you could breathe, they would find you a job to do. Looking back, I realize God was with me protecting every step of the way.

Chapter Two

My Family History

I was born in Waverly, Tennessee on a cold, rainy night. My dad told the story of how he walked to town to get Dr. H. Capps to come to the home to deliver me.

My father belonged to the wealthiest family in town, yet he did not own a car. I am not sure why.

My grandfather owned a lumber and building supply. He was a successful builder, even though he had very little education. He had great difficulties doing his books. He rebuilt the dam in

1913 at Loretta Lynn's Ranch located south of Waverly. It was his first major accomplishment in construction.

The family name is on local buildings. Slayden designed the blocks, and my grandfather made them. The blocks were unique with a design facing on the block. There were very few made because they were too heavy to ship.

My grandfather was a tough man and a strong disciplinarian. He had four sons, none of which were willing to participate in his business. That was a big reason why he sold the business.

Grandfather did not approve of my mom. She was from the "wrong" side of the tracks. He was a bitter man due to his sons not carrying on the family business. So, on his death bed, he "fixed" them all.

The housekeeper, Miss Kate, raised my uncles and me. There was no "hanky panky." He married his housekeeper on his death bed. He was in Vanderbilt Hospital when he married her and two days later, he died. She inherited everything that he had. Ha Ha

All my dad's brothers died directly or indirectly from alcohol. Every man in my family except one. One man never drank a drop in his life.

My father was the town drunk for 15 years after he came back from World War II. His name was Lucian. Lucien (with an "e" instead of an "a") McNabb is on my birth certificate.

Mom was poor and died at the age of 24. She had been married four times and died of tuberculosis in 1937. Her last husband was named Warren. Mom was buried beside her last husband, in-between him and another person. I am not sure who the other person was. (Photo of the McNabb plot in the Wyly Cemetery in Waverly is on page 59.)

She was a small woman, beautiful and very attractive with long black hair. The families were split up when my mom died. When mom died, I was sent to live with mom's side of the family; but that did not work out well. They wanted my dad's money.

At the age of 3, I spent the night with my grandmother on my mother's side, and found her half a pint of white lightning. She was known to have a "nip" every now and then. I drank it all; and the next day, they could not wake me up. They called Dr. Hyram Capps, and he slapped me around and told them I was blind, leaping drunk.

At age 11, Uncle W. "Dub" McNabb gave me alcohol. Not only did he give it to me, he bought it for me on purpose. I drank a little at that age, and drank some as a teenager also. That was part of me getting to be a grown man like the other men. I used to watch my granddad every Saturday drink, get drunk and fall in the creek. The housekeeper would call for us boys to come get our granddad out of the creek.

That night Uncle Dub got me drunk, we lived upstairs where there were three windows on Wyly Street. I hung my head out the window and vomited. My grandfather woke me up and told me at lunch time, the vomit had to be off the roof. Most people would have had a conniption fit. Miss Kate, the housekeeper, brought me a bucket of water and a brush to clean it up.

I was one of the McNabb boys. My uncle thought he should tutor me on what the McNabb boys were supposed to be. We had money, chased girls, but not supposed to marry them. Uncle Dub was never married. He had jet black hair and the women thought he was IT!

My dad was in the military when my mom died. He had a nervous disorder (shell shocked), so he stayed drunk. He was always laughing in his drunken stupor. Everyone wished he could get sober.

Uncle Dubb was found dead between two buildings on Joe Johnson Street in north Nashville. He was in his early 40's when he died. He was buried before I even knew he had passed away. The other brother, William, just drank himself to death. He was in his 50's when he died. One of Uncle William's sons died in a car wreck that was alcohol related. Uncle Dub and Uncle William are buried in the Wyly Cemetery in Waverly, Tennessee. The other brother who never drank, never drove. He ran a grocery store for 60 years. He is buried in Linden, Tennessee.   Family Cemetery

My grandfather died at age 80 from pancreatitis due to alcohol. My grandmother never drank; she died before I was born. My dad died at age 60. He froze to death after he had passed out from alcohol.

Dad never could manage his money because he stayed drunk all the time. He would stay at the taxicab place on Highway 13 south of Waverly and Mr. Bowen would manage his money.

I went to school in Nashville, then Jackson, Tennessee. Then, at age 8, I was back in Waverly to live with my grandfather.

I built model airplanes all my life. I wanted to be a part of flying planes. I had no fear. I have never been scared of anything, no normal types of fear.

After I ran away, I was gone for three years before I called to tell my granddaddy, and he cried. After that, I would come home occasionally.

Chapter Three

Reform School and Penitentiary

In Memphis, at age 14, I went to reform school. I had stolen a car and took it across the state line, which made it a federal offense. Due to this, I was 1-1/2 years in reform school. I went to school while I was there.

One of the ways God looked out for me was every time I was incarcerated, I got educated. I got my GED and some college credits. I always enjoyed learning and kept my nose clean, which thus allowed me to serve only half of my sentence.

First place of incarceration – Federal Reformatory – El Reno, Oklahoma – At age 14, I went to visit a buddy, and his daddy had a 1939 Ford four- door sedan. It started out as a joy ride. I got it started and just kept going. I drove from Trezevant, Tennessee to Oklahoma City, Oklahoma. I drove 600 miles before I got caught. I drove through Memphis, Tennessee. I had little driving experience.

Federal Reformatory El Reno Oklahoma

When I got caught, there was a roadblock for something else and I came upon it. They realized I was only 14 years old, and I went to jail for a year and a half.

17

My friend's daddy came all the way to Oklahoma City to get the car. He called me every name that you could think of. He would have hurt me if he could have. It was downhill from there – I was turned over to the Federal authorities.

Every time I ended up in the pen, I would take advantage of the opportunity to get educated. I got my General Education Degree (GED) and two associates degrees. It was amazing that I even had the desire to get educated. After El Reno Reformatory, I went back to Memphis as an adult. I stayed for one year working then I walked through the doors of the Army Recruiting in 1945. (see Chapter Five)

Second place of incarceration – Federal Penitentiary – Leavenworth, Kansas – I was in the military 3-1/2 years. I got in trouble. I got drunk and hit a guy and took his wallet. I got a Dishonorable Discharge and was sent to Leavenworth Federal Penitentiary. After 1-1/2 years, they found out I was underage and re-did all my paperwork and discharged me. I tried to get my dishonorable discharge removed, since the government messed up my paperwork so bad, but they canceled all my military paperwork so I could not be considered a Veteran.

United States Penitentiary

Leavenworth Kansas

Third place of incarceration – Shelby County Penal Farm –

Memphis, Tennessee due to writing bad checks.

Shelby County Penal Farm
1045 Mullins Station, Memphis, TN, 38134

I was investigated for murder. There was a murder that took

place, and I was going to get the person that did it but instead

went into a drunken stupor. Many of my days and nights were

spent in drunken stupors.

Chapter Four

Marriage and Divorce and Drinking

I got smarter, met my first wife when I was 19 and she was 18. We were passionately in love. We were married in 1949 for 14 years. During that marriage, drinking really started controlling my life. Her family put me in a Gartley-Ramsey Treatment Facility, which used the taper-off method. When I woke up in the hospital, there was a bottle of Jack Daniels and a shot glass. I woke up thinking I was in Heaven – I could not imagine that type of treatment! Their plan was for me to drink some less and less each day for thirty days, trying to taper me off. After the thirty days, they sent me home. This did not work for I went back home to the same lifestyle. I was drinking more when I got out then when I went in.

After two weeks in the facility, one of the orderlies found me under the bed. People were bringing me bottles of booze every day. One of my pilot buddies. I did this for 30 or 35 days, then went back to work.

My wife was an only child, and her parents never dreamed I was an alcoholic. They thought I was cured. They thought I was a fool drinking. They paid $300 per day for 35 days. My family constantly reminded me how I had better straighten up, because they had spent that money on me. This did not bother me one bit. My attitude back then was one of the things that make me realize God had a plan for me. Doctors would tell me I was going to die, but my attitude kept me going.

That lasted one week, then I was drunk again. As the years went by, I went into a mental hospital at the Alcohol Addiction

Division. I was there twice. Both times, I stayed thirty days, then back to the same lifestyle. One time I went two years before going back into treatment.

I woke up one day in an actual gutter on 1026 Poplar Street in Memphis. When I woke up, I realized I had been literally asleep in the gutter. That is about as low as a person can get.

The Gutter in Memphis, TN

It is amazing that no one robbed me! Beer joints closed at 11:00 p.m. back then, but when I woke up, it was daylight. That meant I was laying in the gutter for many hours, but no one bothered me or my belongings or ran over me. I didn't have a bruise. I must have just laid down.

I used to wake up in people's houses and I didn't know how I got there. Everybody loved me and would take me home with them. It's just amazing, after all those years, and I never actually suffered any kind of sickness. Sometimes, I would go a week at a time without taking a bath.

My first wife was good, and I wasn't. She had her eye on a career. She had goals. I had drinking in my mind. During our 14-year marriage, we had five children. She got pregnant six times but had a miscarriage with one. For three years, we never tried to prevent pregnancy, then after three years, it was back-to-back pregnancies. I didn't straighten up.

She went on to become a big shot with Cummings Diesel Engine Company. Her title was National Traffic Director. She ran their Transportation Department and was sent to Europe. When she retired, the company had a party in Manheim, Germany. It took her two weeks to retire due to all the parties.

She made arrangements for that company to have a soft side tractor trailer truck.

When we divorced in 1963, our children were 11, 10, 9, and 8 years of age. We lost the youngest one from crib death. When I got to where I could not fly, I began driving a truck. I spent 40 years doing this. I wanted to be an aviator, and she wanted a career.

Clifton Boyd McNabb, my oldest son, passed away at age 62. He was addicted to food, he had six stints in his heart. He worked for the government and did X-rays for the Veteran's Administration. He had one child, a boy.

My second child is Cheryl Lynn McNabb Moore, my daughter who lives in Munford which is close to Memphis. She works for a place that sells house items and has not been successful in marriage. She has been married twice. Her husband passed away with cirrhosis of the liver from alcohol. She has a son by her first husband. He is a Director of Cocaine Alcohol Awareness Program (CAAP) in Memphis. He's an addict and getting his Doctorate.

My third child is Cynthia Elana McNabb Montoya, age 53. While a schoolteacher for 30 years, she fell at school and thought she was having an inner ear infection, which it was not. She had an infection in her eye that got in her spinal fluid; as a result, she is paralyzed from her waist down. She has three grown children, one is a teacher, one a band director, and one a bell hop.

The first child, Monroe McNabb, lived to be two and a half months and died with SIDS (Sudden Infant Death Syndrome also known as Crib Death).

Two members of our family died with SIDS. My daughter, Cheryl, had a baby who died at the babysitter's house while taking a nap and never woke up.

My second wife's name was Sharon Hall McNabb, also called DeeDee. We had one child, a son, Randall Scott McNabb. He is 46 years old and married with two children.

I have a total of 3 grandchildren, 11 great grandchildren and 1 great-great grandchild.

After the divorce from my first wife, I stayed drunk; and she worked and took care of the children. I was single five years, then I really fell into the pit.

I would like to say that all the years I wallowed in the gutter, all of my drunken stupors, I was never unfaithful to either one of my wives.

Alcohol destroys all sense of responsibility. It made me become the life of the party. If someone planned a party, I was invited because I could tell every dirty joke there was. I loved to dance. I could do everything, but understand, it was killing me.

The parties were daily. I had favorite honky-tonks. They were open from 11 a.m. to 11 p.m. I would stand up at the end of the bar from the time the bar opened until the bar closed. I would go times without a penny to my name, and I wouldn't go a minute without a drink. Someone would always be willing to buy me one. Men would just want a drinking buddy. I could tell jokes and people loved that. I thought if I could stand up, I could drink more all day long. I didn't want to miss anything. I could see the front door and see who came in.

Everyone who came in the front door knew me within minutes. They all knew Buddy McNabb. I physically helped to build a classy bar in downtown Memphis called "The Golden Barrel." I bought the first legal drink they ever sold for a man named Bill Colley. This is also where I met Chris, my second wife.

I was involved in an accident one time while driving a truck that killed three women. It was their fault and from that, I went into a treatment facility due to alcohol. It tore me up really bad.

Highway 66 out of St. Louis, and a four-lane highway coming up straight, three ladies just crossed over into my lane. Her car went under my truck. I used that as an excuse to stay drunk for three months. I went into Gaylord Hospital at that time. I stayed in the facility for thirty days.

In all that time, God was looking out for me and I didn't realize it. I had no raising in the church.

Chapter Five

The Army

I went into the military at the age of 15 on June 13, 1945. I picked up the paperwork right across the street from the park bench. I forged my signature, age, etc. No one asked any questions perhaps because I was taller than most my age and thus appeared older. If you could breathe, and your heart was beating, you could join the army.

I was tickled to pieces! World War II was over shortly after I joined in June, and the war was over in August of 1945. The war in Europe was over, but Japan would not surrender, so President Truman dropped the atomic bomb.

The army assigned me to Old Army Air Corps. All went well through basic training. Booz began entering the picture at the age of 16 when I began drinking.

At age 16, December 10, 1946, I sent a letter to Lurtin McNeil, (who was one of the two boys that was supposed to run away with me when I was 13, but chickened out). He kept that letter for many years.

Lurtin was Humphreys County Sheriff for two terms and was heavy into politics. Tennessee Department Of Correction served under Tennessee Governor Frank G. Clement. He got into trouble about a truck of whiskey, then went to work as an electrician. He was married and had a daughter.

Chapter Six

Flying Career

I obtained my first Pilot's license in 1950. In fact, during that year, I could carry passengers. My first passenger was my first wife. She was not impressed; you could not scare her with dynamite. A guy asked her, "How did he do?" She said, "Okay."

I got my Commercial License in 1951, it was within the same year, and started dusting cotton to kill the boll weevil. In the old days that was an adventurous joy. We wore soft leather helmets, not hard helmets.

We carried 1,900 pounds of dust in the front and could choke a whole lot with that much dust. In the old days, it was sort of a dangerous job; but to us, it was an adventurous joy – and I had a whole lot of alcohol in my veins. It was fun, as well, work. My plan was to be an airline pilot. I applied at Southern Airlines, but they found out about my record.

I dusted cotton in the morning, went to flight school at night, then I would go get drunk. I slept two or three hours, then I would hit the field again.

This photo below is not the actual plane I flew, but it is a plane dusting cotton.

I would have been sitting in the right seat as co-pilot, but in 1952, I ended up in my first treatment facility at Gartley-Ramsey Hospital. This was a private treatment facility.

Chapter Seven

It's a Matter of Faith

It's the closest to God.

You can climb 30,000-foot-high mountains and still be standing on the ground. When you jump out of a plane, there is no ground. If you are a person of faith, you realize that's as close to God as you can be and still be alive.

The first time I parachuted I parachuted out of a plane, (see photo on page 61) I was overwhelmed with the beauty. There is nothing that I have ever seen that will compare. It's simply God's beauty. We can see the curvature of the earth. The

Tennessee River looks like a creek but painted blue like a crayon. You can see whole blocks of color.

Buddy McNabb Skydiving

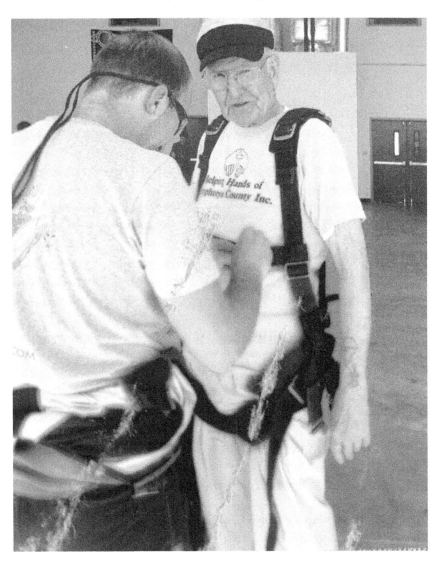

The last time I jumped, it was in the spring, 2016. I was age 86. On the way down, the instructor would see something beautiful and tell me to look. He said we may need to quit doing this and start sitting in a rocking chair on our porch. The scenery was absolutely amazing.

It takes faith to step out of the plane. You get a rush. You never think of it being dangerous. If you ever did, you would never do it again. If you are a person of faith, it's not a concern because if the parachute opens, it's fine. If it doesn't, it's also fine because you know where you are going. The day I made the decision to jump was on my 80th birthday after asking my wife, Chris, if she would jump with me. I knew when she spoke in a certain tone of voice and said no, I knew better than to ask her again. She was supportive of me, and did come to watch me jump, but she didn't want to jump. She knew my faith.

Four days before she died, she laid 31 days without food. Brother Thad Collier, Pastor of Waverly United Methodist

Church, was leaning over talking to her. She looked up at him

and said, "I'm going to see Jesus" and had a smile on her face.

Chapter Eight

The Musician

I am a musician. One of the very first country music drummers. I was a staff musician for Hi label. All recording companies have back up producers, and put their own people in.

I played with some pretty famous folks and got drunk with some pretty famous folks. I played behind Webb Pierce, George Jones, and other famous ones – We would spend a week at a time being drunks. We would spend days and nights where he, Webb Pierce, could hide.

Webb was a big-time country music singer. I played behind a lot of bands. The Texas Playboys was a group I played with one night.

I played with the band leader for Austin City Limits. I once saw it on television, and it was as if history rolled back. During that time, I played lots of music, drank a lot of liquor, chased a lot of girls – the things that drunks do.

Chapter Nine

My Second Wife

When I met Chris Hall, she drove up to a bar where I was on a motorcycle, came in and took her helmet off. She had her red hair flowing down. I turned to Bob Honore and said, "Who in the world is that?" He knew her because he was there all the time. She was an English major student on her way to Memphis State University. We were together for the rest of our lives. She had dark blue eyes and beautiful red hair. Before Bob could tell me anything else about her, I was at the bar standing right beside her.

The whole Bible is about teaching us to love one another and have faith. It is simple, but we try to complicate things.

Christianity is not complicated. We just make it that way. People get excited and think things should be their way, but it's not necessarily that way to everyone.

So many things have happened to me.

When Chris and I first met, I stayed drunk for ten years. For five years, we did not even have a place to stay. We stayed on people's couches, slept in the back seats of cars, we camped out, we would get a little money and then rent an efficiency apartment for a month or two until we got kicked out. We lived off of love (so to speak). We were together for three months when I went into treatment. It was my fourth time, but first time since being with her.

She went to work at Baptist Hospital in Memphis and worked there for 30 years. When Chris first started, she was a waitress in the hospital then, went into the business office and became the probate clerk. After I retired, she then transferred to

Huntingdon Baptist as the Emergency Room Supervisor, then she retired.

I have been blessed with a great personality and have always made people happy. My wife loved that I had been in the music industry. She was 13 years younger than I and was a college student when we met. She thought I "hung the moon."

The tool that God used to make me "clean up my act" was to put a fear in me that I would lose her.

A few days before I went into treatment for the last time, my wife made the comment that she hated me. I had never heard her say that before. It tore me up. She never said that but one time. I went into the care unit and as of 2020, I have been sober 47 years.

I had a particular incident happen to me. I had a guy two days after my coming out of the Care Unit came to my house with a half-gallon of booze. I trembled and sweated, and I told him he could "come in, but his jug couldn't."

That was the real turning point. My friend cussed me, left and he died shortly after that. We never spoke again.

I kept my friends but quit drinking with them. I have one friend left alive, Bob Honore. His wife is 93 years old and still plays bridge three days per week. He writes wild letters to the no-longer-in-print Commercial Appeal newspaper in Memphis.

I do have a few friends that were wives of my friends who are still alive. They are shocked when I call them that I'm still alive.

If I could go back to the day when I ran away, I would do the same thing.

I have a sixth-grade education, spoke to Governors, awards by Governors, Lawyers, Indian Chiefs, and I can speak to anyone. God has blessed me. If I had not been led by God, I would not even have sought after my education. God had a plan. He gave me a message from my mess.

I received Volunteer of the Year Award for Humphreys County in 2014 by Governor William Edward Haslam.

Banquet for the Volunteer of the Year Award

I met an Indian Chief when I managed the Humphreys County Airport. He was the head of the eastern part of the Cherokee Nation. A bigwig would fly into the airport and they would have a ritual, then they talked about Cherokee affairs, which is when I "shot the bull" with them.

Buddy McNabb Airport Manager

Tried retirement three times. I would sit and watch Chris go to work. I began going to the gym. Someone mentioned the United Way, and there I met Susan Goodman, then the head of the Humphreys County United Way. I became her assistant. I assisted with the Food Pantry. When Susan heard me talk about jumping out of the airplane, she grabbed me, and I went

with her to various companies. I would tell those in attendance

about jumping out of planes and hunger for food.

Chapter Ten

Times When God Was With Me

In the middle of my drinking, I ran with a not-so-good group of people (drunks). There was a group of brothers named the Tiller's in Memphis. The youngest Tiller (Mike) was a wimp. All the others were Golden Gloves (boxing). Mike would snitch on others to the police. He developed his own group. He and his group beat up a crippled man. Two other guys and I went to kill him, but God protected me by not letting me find him because I would have killed him. They all hung out at five beer joints, and basically lived there.

Not long after that, his uncle killed him and, cut him up in little pieces. They never did find all of his body parts. His uncle went

50

to prison and stayed in prison until he died about three years ago.

As mentioned on page 15, I had stolen that car when I was 13. I didn't know how to drive, but I drove from Trezevant, Tennessee all the way to Oklahoma City.

God directed the police officer when I first arrived in Memphis not to take me to jail when he found me asleep on the park bench at age 13. He allowed me to sleep on the couch and helped me get a job. My grandfather cried when I called him at age 22. I came home the next time.

At age 15, I went to prison. They thought I was an adult (1943). I beat a guy up and stole from him. It was on Federal property, that's why I went to prison. Three cells down was "Foots" Odom, a member of Machine Gun Kelly's gang. When a young boy goes to prison, they get raped. The day I checked in, "Foots" introduced himself to me. Not one inmate bothered me at all. God protected me.

On July 11, 2018, I was involved in a two-car accident out on Highway 13 in front of Loretta Lynn's Ranch south of Waverly. I was doing a kind deed taking a lady to get her prescriptions. I carried a lady friend with me because I do not want to put myself in a position of transporting young women alone.

As we were driving down the highway, a lady ran a stop sign and drove right out in front of me.

She knocked me over into another car, and I was going head on into on-coming traffic. I'm not sure exactly how God allowed that on-coming car to miss me, but he did. I got out of the car and was praying and thanking God and the other people there probably thought I was crazy, but that's okay. God had angels all around us. Both cars were totaled, but not a scratch on any person in both cars. I was 88 years old and the lady's mother who was in our vehicle with us was 84. Neither of us were sore. All five of us were perfectly fine. My friend was suspended in the air and the seat belt kept her in place. "I will strengthen them in the Lord and in his name they will live securely," declares the Lord. (Zechariah 10:12 NIV)

Thank you, Lord!

After the wreck, one guy walked up to me and started to talk but he had a blank look on his face. He knew I was praying. He was in shock that I was praying.

I am a quiet person, talking to God 40 times a day, but I don't normally pray verbally in front of a crowd. My friend, "Candy" Miller and I were having dinner one time, and I was quietly praying over our food. When I opened my eyes, there was a family standing around us.

I believe God has divine appointments.

I am a simple Christian man. I don't think of myself as being a preacher. It's a personal relationship. God's been there my whole life. I just didn't have sense enough to know it.

I was 38 years old when I married Chris. I accepted Jesus in my heart. I was married to Chris 51 years. I met a pastor once a week.

Chapter Eleven

I Should Have Died or Been Seriously Injured

There were so many times in my younger life when I should have died or been seriously injured.

At the age of 14, I met some people that I was working with that were older than I. They drank pretty heavy, so I joined in. One invited me to his home in Trezevant, Tennessee, for a family get together. There was eating, drinking and playing music, and we had lots of fun. There was also a neat little 1939 four-door Ford Sedan, a really sharp car. I had personally very little driving experience at this time in my life, but at 1 a.m., I crawled out of a window and stole the car. I made it all the way to Oklahoma before I got caught.

This was the beginning of my life of crime. They brought me back to Memphis and tried me in Federal Court and sentenced me to three years in the Federal Reformatory in El Reno Oklahoma (details on page 16). I served one year and was sent back to Memphis and placed on probation. This arrangement lasted about six months. Then, one night while partying big time - and of course, drinking big time - I ran out of money. So, I beat up one of the guys who was partying with us and took his money. I was caught shortly thereafter, and since this crime took place on government property, I was sentenced to 30 years in the Federal Penitentiary at Leavenworth, Kansas (details on page 17). They sent me back to Memphis and put me on probation again. There I continued to live a wild lifestyle. I worked, I drank, I partied.

I always had a great love for airplanes, even as a small child, I used to build models. So, at about the age of 18, I started learning to fly. By 19, I had a commercial pilot's license. I had a short flying career as a commercial pilot that lasted about three years. During those three years, I was an agricultural pilot (duster pilot) which is very dangerous flying. During those three years, I saw several people killed and several people injured flying dusters.

Many times, I had to be helped up into the airplane because I would be drunk when I went to work. My boss used to tell the other guys, "Don't worry about Buddy, he can fly the crates the airplanes came in." And in the three years, I never put a scratch on an airplane or myself.

During that time, my first wife's family put me in treatment twice, but it didn't work. Finally, after 14 years of misery, she kicked me out. I remained single five years and continued to drink heavily, but managed to work enough to support myself.

As time went by, I met another wonderful young lady fresh out of college, we fell in love immediately, got married, and were together for 51 years. Notice I did not say happily together. I continued to drink the first ten years we were together. Finally, after six times in treatment, I learned to stay sober. After six years of sobriety, I started attending church with my wife.

Our preacher at that time was an old country boy named Charles Leist. Brother Charles played guitar and banjo. I played mandolin. We had lots of sessions. After each session, Brother Charles would preach to me a tiny bit. It finally worked. Forty-three years ago, which would have been 1977, I gave my life to the Lord, and I've walked with him ever since. I immediately started to realize that God had walked with me everyday of my life because he had a long-term plan for my life; and in these many years, he has put me in many positions to help people that he wanted helped.

After many years of trucking, I retired. This did not work! I decided to buy a dump truck. Mom (nickname for my wife, Chris), being the level-headed one, asked if I could drive a dump truck. I answered brilliantly, "Of course, if it has wheels on it," but she suggested I try driving someone else's dump truck before we invest $100,000 or more. I followed her advice and got a job driving for someone else. After several months, I rolled the truck over, but once again, I didn't get a scratch. It scared Mom real bad. So much for being a dump truck driver. So, I was sitting on the porch again watching Mom go to work. It was driving me up the wall!

We had a neighbor down the road who worked at Turney Center Penitentiary. She suggested I go out and work at the penitentiary. I told her I was 69 years old and that they were not going to hire anybody that old. She said they would. I said they wouldn't. They did. I worked at Turney Center Penitentiary for six and a half years. I learned a lot about human nature, about good and evil, and witnessed many, many blessings.

Mom went home to be with Jesus on February 21, 2015. I miss her, but I know where she is, and I will see her again someday. On her death bed, she whispered to a dear friend of ours, "Help Buddy be involved with the church." It seems that since Mom's passing, God continuously presents me with opportunities to help troubled people.

As I have lived this life, considering the good, the bad, the ugly, it has become obvious to me that God had a plan from day one of my life.

In order to teach me to do the things that he wants me to do, he let Satan send me,

"To Hell and Back in a Bottle."

THE END

Buddy McNabb

ISBN: 9798698799603

Made in the USA
Coppell, TX
24 August 2021

61067687R00036